AF316709

THE TWO KOREAS

HOW THE NORTH SEPARATED FROM THE SOUTH

Geography History Books
Children's Geography & Cultures Books

Speedy Publishing LLC

40 E. Main St. #1156

Newark, DE 19711

www.speedypublishing.com

Copyright 2017

In this book, we're going to cover how and why North Korea and South Korea separated from each other. So, let's get right to it!

A BRIEF HISTORY OF KOREA

Korea, both north and south, has been inhabited for over 10,000 years. Scientists think that the ancestors of modern Koreans came from the regions of Siberia as well as Mongolia. The history of Korea has been one of lands that have been divided, reunited, divided again, and fighting with each other for many centuries.

Gyeongbokgung Palace

Korea's very first kingdom was called **Old Chosun**. For more than 20 centuries, it had domain over the northwest part of the country as well as parts of China. In 108 BC, it was grabbed up by the Chinese. They divided the area into three new kingdoms,

named Silla, Paekche, and Koguryo. Many centuries later in 660 AD, the Silla kingdom, with the aid of Chinese troops, gained control of what was known as Korea at that time.

Wang Kon

By 901 AD, the kingdom was once again broken up into three different kingdoms. A powerful leader by the name of Wang Kon brought the country back to unified rule and named the new kingdom Koryo. This kingdom lasted from 936-1392 AD. Then the Yi family grabbed control over the throne and began the dynasty that was later called the Choson dynasty. They ruled Koryo until 1910.

THE EUROPEANS COME TO KOREA

A merchant ship crashed into Jeju Island off the coast of what is now known as South Korea in the year 1656. These sailors were the first Europeans to see Korea. They were captured and remained prisoners there for 13 years. Only one of the sailors escaped.

Merchant Ship on Jeju Island

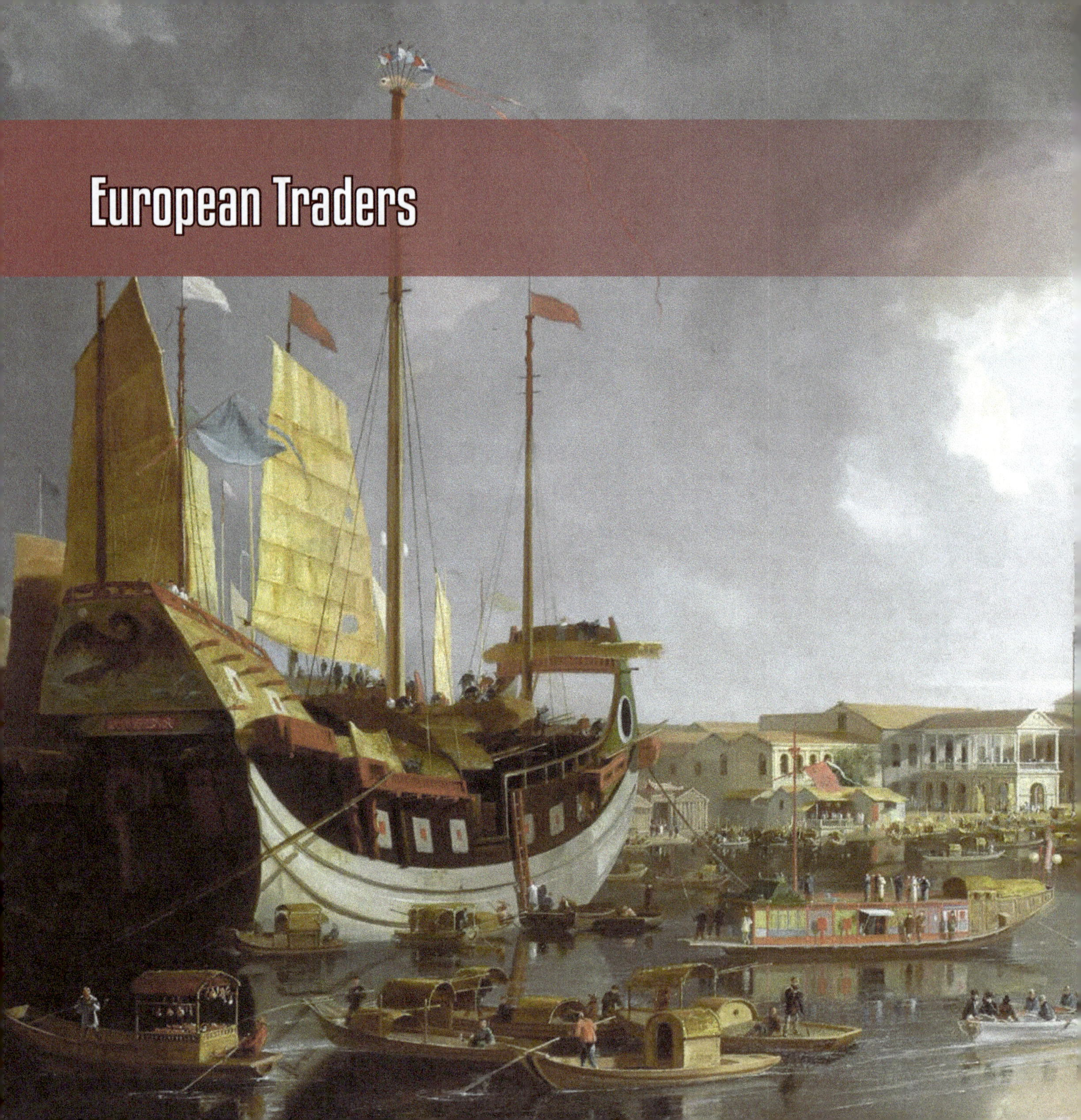
European Traders

Upon his return to Europe, he told stories of the beautiful lands and resources, which inspired European traders with a desire to see the country. However, European ships weren't allowed in Korea's ports until the dawn of the 19th century.

JAPAN ANNEXES KOREA

Geographically, both Japan and China are situated close to Korea. In 1894, there was a major uprising in Korea. Both the Japanese and Chinese sent troops to stop the unrest. After this action, both countries as well as Russia fought for domain over Korea.

A Procession in Seoul

By 1904, Russia and Japan were still fighting over who was to maintain control over Korea. Japan won the battle and took the country in 1910 after installing a leader by the name of Sunjong. He was the last emperor to preside over the entire country of Korea, but, by this time, Korea was unified in name only.

When Sunjong died in 1926, the Japanese government was in complete control of Korea. They wanted the Koreans to adopt the Japanese culture. They tried to suppress Korea's language and traditions. They created a law that the citizens needed to use Japanese last names. Due to these actions, many Koreans are anti-Japanese, even today.

A Korean Palace with Japanese
Architectural Design

THE END OF WORLD WAR II

Prior to World War II, Hitler had made a pact with Stalin that the two countries of Germany and Russia wouldn't attack each other. The Axis Powers consisted of Nazi Germany, as well as Italy and Japan. At the beginning, Great Britain and France were the only ones fighting the Nazis.

When the Japanese attacked Pearl Harbor in December of 1941, the United States joined the anti-Nazi effort. So, in addition to the United States, the major Allied Powers included Great Britain, France, China, and the Soviet Union.

Japanese torpedo attack on "Battleship Row"
Pearl Harbor

The Big Three Allied Leaders

Russia had wanted to join the Axis Powers to begin with, but Hitler had not allowed that to occur. Despite their previous pact, Hitler invaded the Soviet Union and they then joined the Allies. Even though the United States and the Soviet Union were on the same side against Hitler and Nazi Germany, it was an uneasy alliance since the US is a democratic government and the Soviet Union was a communist government.

The Allied Forces won the war
and Japan lost its territories
including Korea. The Soviet
Union had troops in North
Korea and the United States
had troops in South Korea.
The two countries were
divided at the 38th parallel.

Japanese torpedo attack on "Battleship Row"
Pearl Harbor

NORTH DIVIDED FROM SOUTH

Due to the Soviet Union, the North now had a communist government, while the South was anti-communist. Now that World War II was over, the military tension between the Soviet Union and the United States became the "Cold War."

By 1949, two new governments had been created on the peninsula. In the North, Kim Il Sung was a communist dictator who was backed by the Soviet government. In the south, the US government stood by the dictator Syngman Rhee. Although the South didn't have a democracy, they were anti-communism.

A
Military
Demarcation
Line
MZ)
2nd Tunnel
4th Tunnel
st Tunnel
Tunnel
SOUTH
KOREA

U.S. ARMY

Tensions were running high between the Soviet Union and the United States and likewise between North and South Korea. Neither dictator wanted to stay on his side of the border. Battles were breaking out all the time and before the Korean War started almost 10,000 soldiers from both sides were killed.

THE KOREAN WAR

In June of 1950, the war in Korea started when over 75,000 North Korean soldiers and 150 tanks started coming across the 38th parallel, which was the boundary between the two countries. The Cold War had now started an aggressive military action. The Soviet Union stayed "behind the scenes" although it was clear they were behind the war.

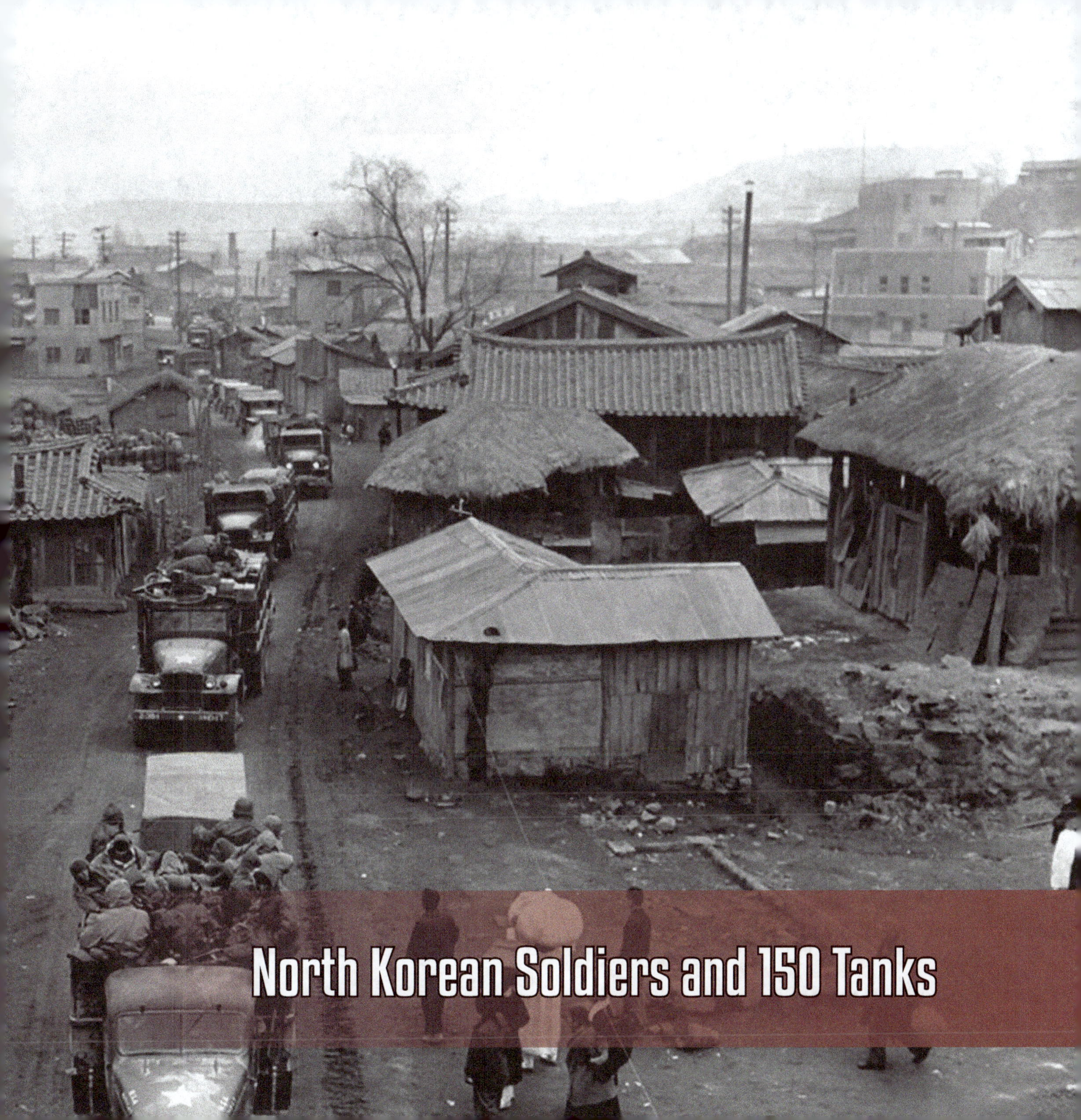
North Korean Soldiers and 150 Tanks

The Chinese and North Koreans were the ones actively fighting. However, the Soviet Union had trained the North Korean army and provided them with supplies.

This aggressive invasion was a surprise to US government officials, but they felt there was no choice. The National Security Council had recommended earlier that year in a report that the US do everything possible to stop communism from expanding.

By July, America had entered the war. From a global perspective, this battle wasn't just about two unstable dictators. It was about whether the communists would be able to grab up lands and topple democracy as a way of life. The fight had become a fight between good and evil the way Americans looked at it.

After some initial battles back and forth across the dividing line, the fighting was resulting in thousands of casualties but no decisive victories. Officials in the US worked hard to put some type of armistice into position. They were concerned that this conflict would erupt into a war with Russia or China. Such a war could easily have escalated into World War III and nuclear destruction.

WAR STRATEGIES

At first the strategy was merely to push the communists out of South Korea. The army of North Korea was very well trained and well supplied. In contrast, the South Korean forces seemed confused and reluctant to fight. It was a very hot, dry summer and American troops didn't have enough water.

American Troops

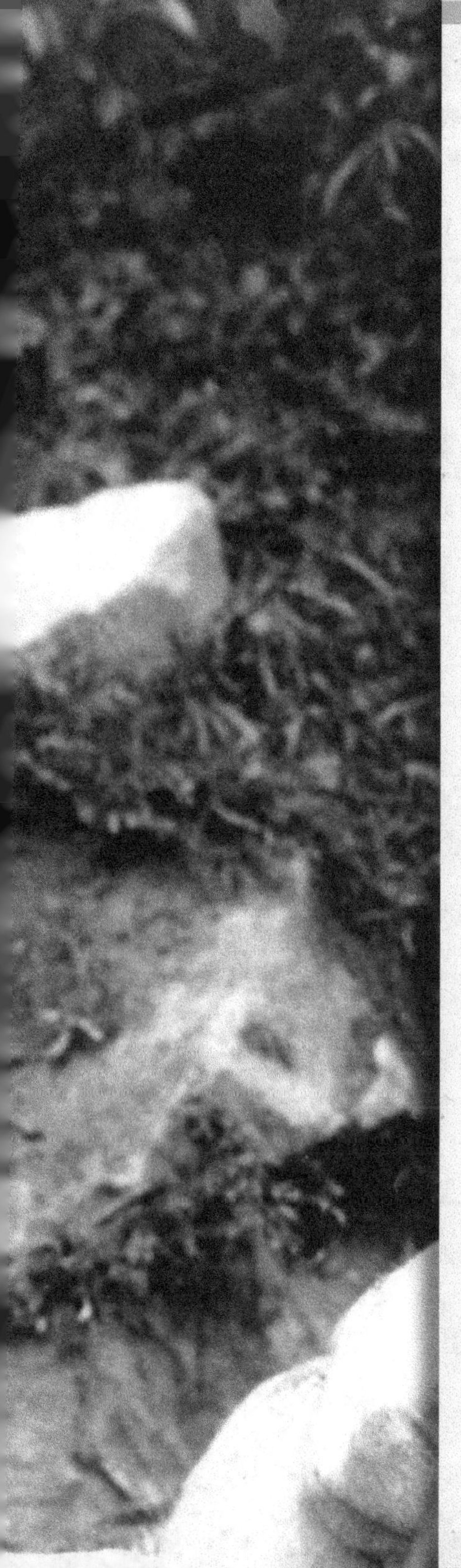

The thirsty soldiers drank the only water that was available in standing rice paddies. The water was contaminated with human waste so many became ill with abdominal pain.

By the end of the summer, US president Truman and Douglas MacArthur, his general, had decided to take a more aggressive approach. They would work to free the North from communist rule.

General McArthur, South Korea

The United States pushed the North Koreans out of the city of Seoul and back to the northern side of the 38th parallel. However, as US soldiers started to approach the border between Northern Korea and China, the Chinese leader Mao Zedong sent troops to fortify North Korea. He issued a warning to the United States to stay away unless they wanted to engage China in all out war.

NO SUBSTITUTE FOR VICTORY

President Truman did not want to go to war with the Chinese government. It would surely mean a full-scale nuclear war and millions of deaths worldwide.

President Truman

General MacArthur

However, General MacArthur did not agree. He felt that there was "no substitute for a full victory" against communism in all its forms. Fearing that MacArthur would single-handedly begin a larger war, Truman fired him.

It took two years of negotiations for an armistice to be signed. By this time, a new president, President Dwight Eisenhower was in office. A final armistice to end the conflict was signed in July of 1953. A two-mile zone was created to provide a buffer between the two countries so that war wouldn't break out again. A peace treaty was never signed, so technically the war was never over.

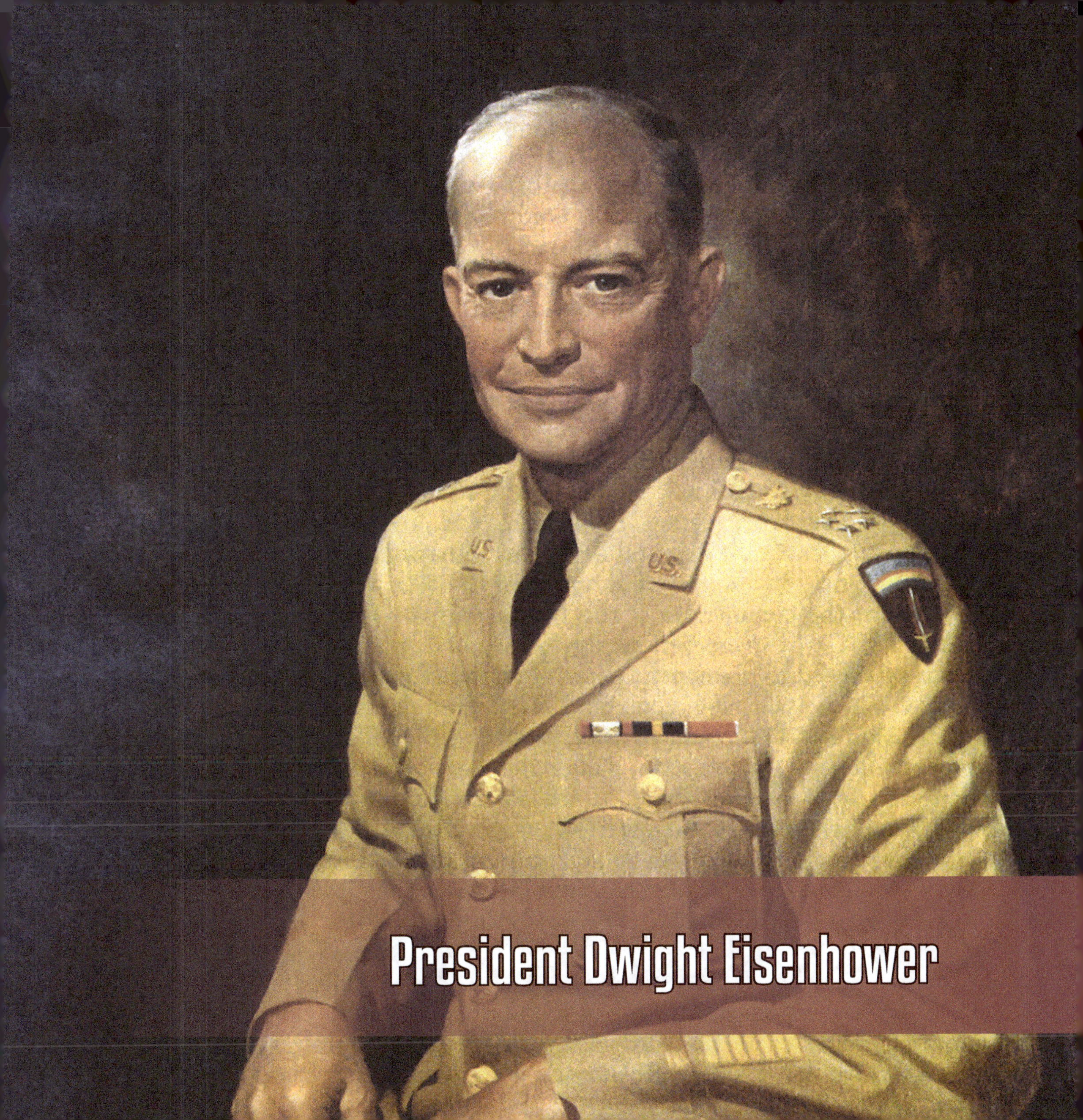
President Dwight Eisenhower

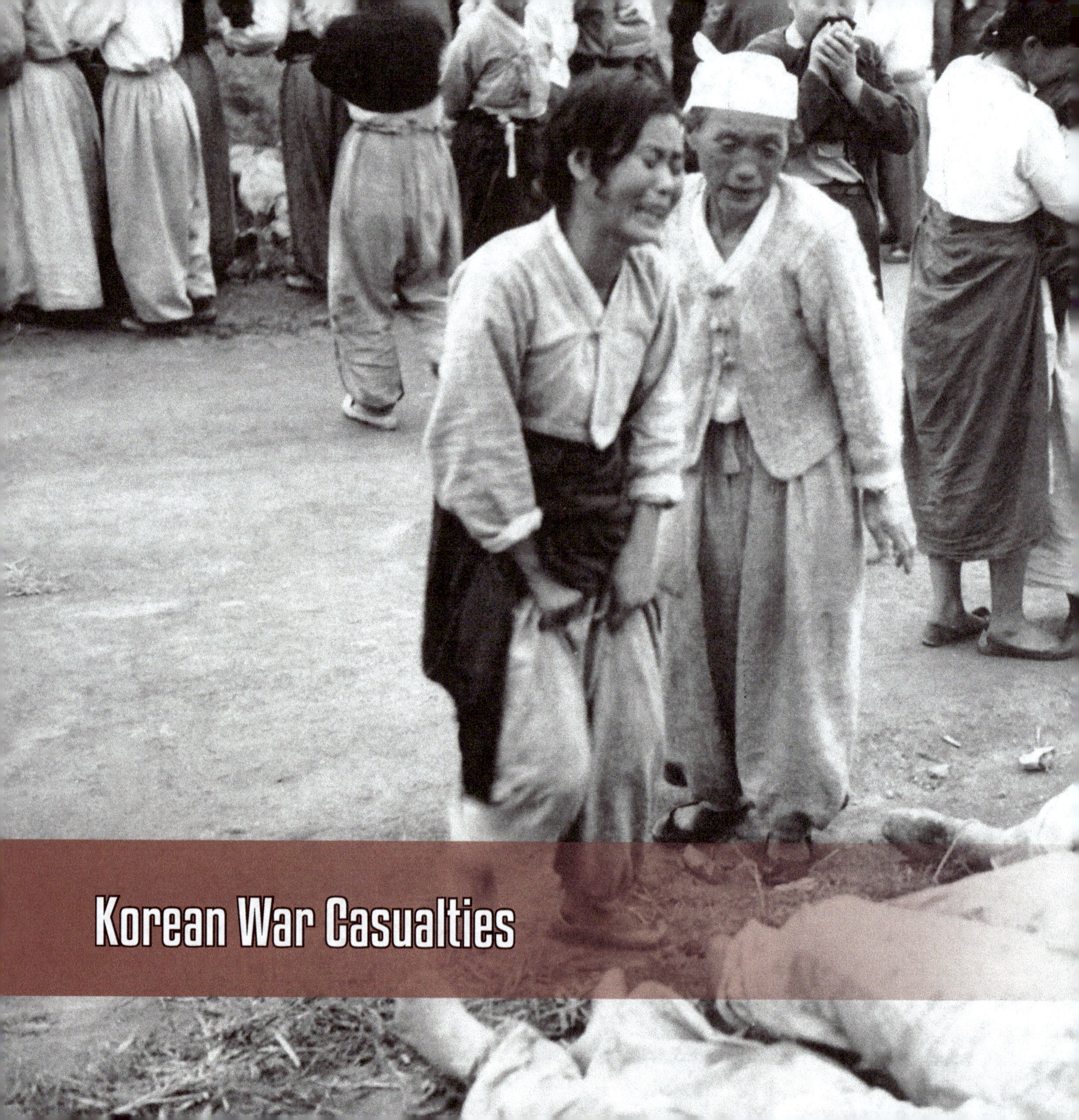

Korean War Casualties

Although the Korean War was short, it caused many casualties. Millions of people died and more than half of the deaths were just ordinary citizens. Ten percent of Korea's population died. Over 35,000 US soldiers died in the conflict and over 90,000 were wounded in this bloody war. The war cost the US government almost $70 million dollars as well.

The conflict and unrest between North and South Korea has continued through today.

Now you know more about the history of North and South Korea and why these two countries are still enemies. You can find more Geography and History Books from Baby Professor by searching the website of your favorite book retailer.

Visit

BABY PROFESSOR
EDUCATION KIDS

www.BabyProfessorBooks.com

to download Free Baby Professor eBooks
and view our catalog of new and exciting
Children's Books